grace

Feb. 10th, 2020

Dear Alism

Your Courage and
Strength is an
inspiration.
Wishing you all
the Best Always

Praveena & Theresa
Geider

grace

QUOTES & PASSAGES FOR
HEART, MIND, AND SOUL

EDITED BY B.C. ARONSON

RANDOM HOUSE REFERENCE

NEW YORK   TORONTO   LONDON   SYDNEY   AUCKLAND

for tod

"THE LOVE OF
A GOOD HUSBAND
PROVIDES GRACE
IN LIFE."

contents

introduction

Try this: Ask several of your friends what "grace" means to them. Guaranteed, each one will have a different interpretation. There is divine grace that manifests itself in the love and mercy of God. There is the grace that we bestow on each other through forgiveness, kindness, and courtesy. There is the grace of style and elegance—as in growing old gracefully. Then there is the grace of movement or action.

One motivation to offer a book about grace is that grace (in any form) seems to be in such short supply in today's world. Read a newspaper or turn on the television and you'll see little evidence that compassion, courtesy, and kindness even exist. Look what happens in parking lots when two cars experience a near miss. Look what happens in restaurants when the wrong food is brought to the table. Indeed, most of us are so busy or stressed that there seems to be little time for grace—that is, to reflect on or receive God's grace, to give grace or to receive the grace of others, or to live and act with grace in everyday life. It's a loss because grace is one of the best things about life.

That's exactly why I took the time to prepare this book of more than three hundred quotations that touch on grace in all its dimensions. The excerpts come from people in all walks of life—spiritual and business leaders, writers and politicians, and even comedians. I hope readers will take a minute or two every day to flip through the pages and find a quote that inspires them and makes them reflect on all the ways grace *does* exist. I hope the insights in this book will also help readers cultivate more grace in their lives. Yes, there is hope for grace in our world today.

For instance, I see grace every day at a local hospital where I am a volunteer. There's the surgeon who comes out of the operating room to talk to a waiting family and introduces himself by his first name, not "doctor," putting the family immediately at ease. There's the emergency room nurse who, although extremely busy, takes the time to hug a frightened and lonely patient. There's the volunteer who drives to the local store to purchase a pretty nightgown (with her own money) for a patient who arrived at the hospital with none of her own clothing. There's the nurse who, although not permitted to wash a patient's hair as a staff member, goes home, changes her clothes, becomes a "regular person," and administers a most-welcome shampoo. There are the hospital staff members who sing "Amazing Grace" at the bedside of a terminally ill patient while the family says good-bye and life support is disconnected.

Then there are the little everyday acts of grace that usually go by unnoticed. They even happen in what one thinks of as the least gracious city in North America: New York City. New York (and other urban areas) seem so aggressive, competitive, and efficient that there can't possibly be time for grace. But you'd be surprised. I remember one hot, sultry summer day when my husband and I were walking near Times Square trying to mind the traffic and traffic lights without getting run over, or at least getting honked at or verbally assaulted. At one intersection, the light had changed just as we were stepping off the curb and we automatically backed up to let traffic through. We looked up and saw two rather ferocious-looking individuals in the front seat of a decrepit white van. We thought for sure they were going to display a rude gesture as they raced through the intersection. However, the driver smiled and waved us through in front of him. We also smiled and waved as we dashed across the street, most grateful for the unexpected moment of grace.

Leaf through *Grace* and see if something strikes a chord. In what ways has grace touched you, and in what ways could you demonstrate grace toward others? Grace has everything to do with the Golden Rule: treat others just as you would like to be treated. And who doesn't want to be treated with grace?

what is grace?

Grace takes on many forms.
For some, grace is forgiveness and
kindness. For others, grace is elegance
and class. For those who are religious,
grace means God's grace, a state of
love and mercy. For all, grace
represents a state of being that
transcends the ordinary and makes
us more understanding, more
loving, and more dignified.

Grace isn't a little prayer you chant
before receiving a meal. It's a way to live.

—*Jackie Windspear, writer*

⬦

Grace means the free, unmerited, unexpected
love of God, and all the benefits, delights, and
comforts which flow from it. It means that while
we were sinners and enemies we have been
treated as sons and heirs.

—*R. P. C. Hanson, scholar*

Grace is the unfailing commitment to love all persons, regardless of their beliefs. Only grace makes it possible for those who believe differently to respect and relate to one another. Grace allows us to disagree, to challenge the damaging beliefs of others even as we are challenged and to do this without violating the autonomy and dignity of others. Grace empowers us to embrace deeply divergent convictions even as we embrace one another. We love one another as God loves us—graciously.

—*Philip Gulley and James Mulholland, writers*

Grace must find expression in life, otherwise it is not Grace.

—*Karl Barth, theologian*

Grace means more than gifts. In grace something is transcended, once and for all overcome. Grace happens in spite of something; it happens in spite of separateness and alienation. Grace means that life is once again united with life, self is reconciled with self. Grace means accepting the abandoned one. Grace transforms fate into a meaningful vocation. It transforms guilt to trust and courage. The word grace has something triumphant in it.

—*Yrjö Kallinen, philosopher and writer*

Catholics think of grace as a supernatural power which God dispenses, primarily through the Church and its sacraments, to purify the souls of naturally sinful human beings, and render them capable of holiness. . . . Protestants think of grace as an attribute of God rather than a gift from God. It is a shorthand term signifying God's determination to love, forgive, and save His human children, however little they deserve it.

—Louis Cassels, religious columnist

<><>

Grace is what God gives us when we don't deserve and mercy is when God doesn't give us what we do deserve.

—Anonymous

Grace in the theological sense is that force that infuses our lives, that keeps letting us off the hook. It is unearned and gratuitous love; the love that goes before, that greets us on the way. It's the help you receive when you have no bright ideas left, when you are empty and desperate and have discovered that your best thinking and most charming charm have failed you; grace is the light or electricity or juice or breeze that takes you from that isolated place and puts you with others who are as startled and embarrassed and eventually grateful as you are to be there.

—*Anne Lamott, writer*

Grace is not returning an upright finger greeting when you have (rightfully) beat someone through the intersection.

—Anonymous

This is how I define grace: You're on the main stage, and it looks like it has been rehearsed one hundred times, everything goes so smoothly. That's where I get my confidence and success, from knowing that I have an edge because I know I'm prepared. You aren't scared of taking a test when you are ready for it. My first couple of years, I was just kind of swimming, trying not to drown, but now. . . .

—Alex Rodriguez, professional
major league baseball player and
All Star player of the year

I'm becoming more and more myself
with time, I guess that's what grace is, the
refinement of your soul through time.

—Jewel, singer and songwriter

⬥

I guess grace doesn't have to [be] logical.
If it did, it wouldn't be grace.

—Max Lucado, writer

soul

Grace touches the soul, the vital principle or animating force within living beings. It is there where a person's innermost emotions and feelings reside. Grace redeems the soul and makes forgiveness and mercy possible. Grace is a spiritual awakening. It's a moment of transcendence. In many religions grace is regarded as a gift from God, given freely, always, without.

Grace is the natural state of every Son of God. When he is not in a state of grace, he is out of his natural environment and does not function well. Everything becomes a strain because he was not created for the environment he has made. He therefore cannot adapt to it, nor can he adapt it to him. There is no point in trying. A Son of God is happy only when he knows he is with God.

—*Marianne Williamson, writer*

✦

It is the grace of God that helps those who do everything that lies within their power to achieve that which is beyond their power.

—*Abraham Joshua Heschel, philosopher and theologian*

True liberation comes through grace
and not through free will.

—Nicolas Berdyaev,
theologian and religious philosopher

❖

The *Thou* meets me through grace—
it is not found by seeking.

—Martin Buber, Judaic scholar and philosopher

The daily bread of grace, without which
nothing can be achieved, is given to
the extent to which we ourselves
give and forgive.

—Aldous Huxley, writer

We need grace in order to be able to live in such a way as to qualify ourselves to receive grace.

—*Aldous Huxley, writer*

❖

Spiritual grace cannot be received continuously or in its fullness, except by those who have willed away their self-will to the point of being able truthfully to say, "Not I, but God in me."

—*Aldous Huxley, writer*

Amazing Grace! How sweet the sound that saved a wretch like me! I once was lost, but now am found, was blind, but now I see. 'Twas Grace that taught my heart to fear, and Grace my fears relieved; How precious did that Grace appear the hour I first believed. Through many dangers, toils, and snares I have already come; 'Tis Grace hath brought me safe thus far and Grace will lead me home. The Lord has promised good to me. His Word my hope secures; He will my shield and portion be as long as life endures. Yea, when this flesh and heart shall fail, and mortal life shall cease, I shall possess, within the veil, a life of joy and peace.

—John Newton, clergyman and hymn writer

Man by grace is made like unto God,
and a partaker in his divinity and . . .
without grace he I like unto the brute beasts.

—Blaise Pascal, mathematician and philosopher

❖

By grace you have been saved through faith, and
this is not our own doing, it is the gift of God—
not because of works, lest any man should boast.

—St. Paul, Apostle

The breeze of God's grace is blowing continually.
You have to set your sail to catch that breeze.

—*Swami Prabhavananda, monk and writer*

The state of love is the state of grace.

—*N. Sri Ram, Theosophical Society Adyar, India*

❖

God does not refuse grace to those
who do what they can.

—*Medieval Latin saying*

Faith cannot be made: it is in the
truest sense a gift of grace.

—*Carl G. Jung, psychologist and psychiatrist*

❖

If the grace of God miraculously operates, it
probably operates through the subliminal door.

—*William James, psychologist and philosopher*

God hath his mysteries of grace,

Ways that we cannot tell,

He hides them deep, like the secret sleep

Of him he loved so well.

—Cecil Frances Alexander, poet

❖

All writing comes by the grace of God,
and all doing and having.

*—Ralph Waldo Emerson, essayist,
poet, and philosopher*

Thus all below is strength,
and all above is grace.

—John Dryden, poet and dramatist

⬥

Some hae meat and canna eat,
And some would eat that want it;
But we hae meat, and we can eat,
Sae let the Lord be thankit.
Grace before Meat.

—Robert Burns, poet and author,
"The Selkirk Grace"

Grace is available for each of us every day—our spiritual daily bread—but we've got to remember to ask for it with a grateful heart and not worry about whether there will be enough for tomorrow.

—Sarah Ban Breathnach, writer and president and CEO of Simple Abundance, Inc.

Jesus wept; Voltaire smiled. From that divine
tear and from that human smile is derived
the grace of present civilization.

—*Victor Hugo, romantic poet, novelist, and dramatist*

⬖

It is only when you have both divine grace
and human endeavor that you can experience
bliss, just as you can enjoy the breeze of
a fan only when you have both a fan and
the electrical energy to operate it.

—*Sri Sathya Sai Baba, guru*

Laughter is the closest thing
to the grace of God.

—Karl Barth, theologian

⊰◈⊱

This is Daddy's bedtime secret for today:
Man is born broken. He lives by mending.
The grace of God is glue.

—Eugene O'Neill, dramatist

The grace of God means something like: Here is your life. You might never have been, but you are because the party wouldn't have been complete without you. Here is the world. Beautiful and terrible things will happen. Don't be afraid. I am with you. Nothing can ever separate us. It's for you I created the universe. I love you. There's only one catch. Like any other gift, the gift of grace can be yours only if you'll reach out and take it. Maybe being able to reach out and take it is a gift too.

—(Carl) Frederick Buechner, writer

God's Grace can change anybody's fate.

—*Sri Chinmoy, philosopher and spiritual guru*

❖

Grace is but glory begun,
and glory is but grace perfected.

—*Jonathan Edwards, theologian*

One of our newer members, a man named Ken Nelson, is dying of AIDS, disintegrating before our very eyes. He came in a year ago with a Jewish woman who comes every week to be with us, although she does not believe in Jesus. Shortly after the man with AIDS started coming, his partner died of the disease. A few weeks later Ken told us that right after Brandon died, Jesus had slid into the hole in his heart that Brandon's loss left, and had been there ever since. Ken has a totally lopsided face, ravaged and emaciated, but when he smiles, he is radiant. He looks like God's crazy nephew Phil. He says he would gladly pay any price for what he has now, which is Jesus, and us.

There is a woman in the choir named Ranola who is large and beautiful and jovial and black and as devout as can be, who has been a little standoffish with Ken. She has always looked at him with confusion, when she looks at him at all. Or she looks at him sideways, as if she wouldn't have to quite see him if she didn't look at him head on. She was raised in the South by Baptists who taught her that his way of life—that he—was an abomination. It is hard for her to break through this. I think she and a few other women at church are, on the most visceral level, a little afraid of catching the disease. But Kenny has come to church almost every week for the last year and won almost everyone over. He finally missed a couple of Sundays when he got too weak, and then a month ago he was back, weighing almost no pounds, his face even more lopsided, as if he'd had a stroke. Still, during the prayers of the people, he talked joyously of his life and his decline, of grace and redemption, of how safe and happy he feels these days.

So on this particular Sunday, for the first hymn, the so-called Morning Hymn, we sang "Jacob's Ladder," which goes, "Every rung goes higher, higher," while ironically Kenny couldn't even stand up. But he sang away sitting down, with the hymnal in his lap. And when it came time for the second hymn, the Fellowship Hymn, we were to sing "His Eye Is on the Sparrow." The pianist was playing and the whole congregation had risen—only Ken remained seated, holding the hymnal in his lap—and we began to sing, "Why should I feel discouraged? Why do the shadows fall?" And Ranola watched Ken rather skeptically for a moment, and then her face began to melt and contort like his, and she went to his side and bent down to lift him—lifted up this white rag doll, this scarecrow. She held him next to her, draped over and against her like a child while they sang.

—*Anne Lamott, writer*

We're all stumbling towards the light with varying degrees of grace at any given moment.

—*Bo Lozoff, cofounder of the Human Kindness Foundation*

❖

Augustine said that we were all born into the world of "common grace" [i.e., available to all]. Before one is baptized, or even if one never is, such grace meets one in God's creation. There is grace in the pear tree that blooms and blushes. There is common grace in the sea (that massive cleanliness which we are proceeding to corrupt), in the fact that there was, before we laid hands on it, clean air. Our task is to appreciate that grace.

—*Joseph Sittler, scholar*

You may call God love,
you may call God goodness.
But the best name for God is compassion.

—*Meister Eckhart, theologian, musician,
and medical missionary*

⊰◈⊱

God will pardon me. It's His business.

—*Heinrich Heine, writer and poet*

31

Grace strikes us when we are in great pain and restlessness. . . . Sometimes at that moment a wave of light breaks into our darkness, and it is as though a voice were saying, "You are accepted."

—*Paul Johannes Tillich, philosopher*

The grace of God is in my mind shaped
like a key, that comes from time to time
and unlocks the heavy doors.

—*Donald Swan, unknown*

❖

The will of God will not take you where
the grace of God cannot keep you.

—*Anonymous*

True grace is neither expected nor deserved.

—*Anonymous*

❖

When we come into contact with the
other person, our thoughts and actions
should express our mind of compassion, even if
that person says and does things that are not
easy to accept. We practice in this way until we
see clearly that our love is not contingent
upon the other person being lovable.

—*Thich Nhat Hanh, Buddhist monk and writer*

Sometimes we get so caught up in the future, we forget to take pleasure in what we have. We become so obsessed with "I want, I want, I want," there is no room left to notice that we are already standing neck-deep in grace.

—*Carolyn Hobbs, therapist, writer, and teacher*

I look at the Samurai because they were the artists of their time. What I think struck me when I read Bushido is compassion. "If there's no one there to help, go out and find someone to help." That hit me, because I try to lead my life like that.

—Tom Cruise, actor

When we finally know we are dying, and all other sentient beings are dying with us, we start to have a burning, almost heartbreaking sense of the fragility and preciousness of each moment and each being, and from this can grow a deep, clear, limitless compassion for all beings.

—Sogyal Rinpoche, writer and authority on Buddhist teachings

The grace of God may step in when you don't
lose your head in a clearly desperate situation.

—*Carl G. Jung, psychologist and psychiatrist*

But the Bible says, even though we may
blow it every day, God's mercy is
fresh for us every morning.

—*Kathie Lee Gifford, singer and actor*

How do I love thee? Let me count the ways.
I love thee to the depth and breadth and height
My soul can reach, when feeling out of sight
For the ends of Being and ideal Grace.

—Elizabeth Barrett Browning, poet

❧

I make that one of my practices; I think that's
an intentional meditation in itself. I sit down
quietly, take a deep breath, try to quiet my mind,
quiet my breathing, and now bring the people in
front of me who have created pain for me, and
then bless them and put light around them and
watch them drift away with love.

—Goldie Hawn, actor

My father was very sure about certain matters pertaining to the universe. To him, all good things—trout as well as eternal salvation—come by grace and grace comes by art and art does not come easy.

—*Norman Fitzroy MacLean, writer*

I have been asked on hundreds of times
in my life why God allows tragedy and suffering.
I have to confess that I really do not know the
answer totally, even to my own satisfaction.
I have to accept, by faith, that God is sovereign,
and He is a God of love and mercy and
compassion in the midst of suffering.

—*Billy Graham, evangelist*

heart

While grace in the religious sense
comes from God, we give grace to
each other through heart. How? We show
others kindness, courtesy, compassion, and
forgiveness. Grace is the driver who lets
you in front of him in heavy traffic. Grace is
the fellow shopper who holds the door open
for you when your arms are loaded with
packages. Grace is the neighbors who bring
food to your doorstep when you are sick or
you have lost a loved one. Grace is the friend
who forgives you for backing into her car.

Shall we make a new rule of life from tonight:
always to try to be a little
kinder than is necessary?

—*J. M. Barrie, writer (*Peter Pan*)*

❖

Kindness can become its own motive.
We are made kind by being kind.

—*Eric Hoffer, social writer*

What is it to practice benevolence?
It is to imitate the Deity.

—Publius Syrus, Ancient Latin writer

❖

Deeds of kindness are equal in weight
to all the commandments.

—Talmud

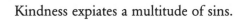

Kindness expiates a multitude of sins.

—*Anonymous*

Grace arrives, unannounced, in lives that least expect or deserve it. . . . Every day we have smaller, calmer chances to turn another's life around, to serve, to listen. How often do we simply not see what is in front of us? How often do we believe that the world's evils—from terrorism to crime to emotional cruelty—are beyond our capacity to change? Or that there is no one in front of us whom we can serve?

—*Andrew Sullivan, essayist and blogger,*
IN "WHEN GRACE ARRIVES UNANNOUNCED—
TIED UP BY A VIOLENT FUGITIVE, ASHLEY SMITH FOUND A
WAY TO LET THE LIGHT IN," ABOUT A VICTIM WHO SAVES
HERSELF FROM A VIOLENT FUGITIVE, AND IN THE
PROCESS SAVES HIM.

Never refuse to do a kindness unless the act would work great injury to yourself, and never refuse to take a drink—under any circumstances.

—*Mark Twain, humorist, writer, and lecturer*

❖

The best happiness insurance is kindness. The premiums are thoughtfulness.

—*Arnold Glasow, writer*

It's nice to be important but
more important to be nice.

—*Anonymous (seen on a sign in
Kutztown, Pennsylvania)*

✦

The thoughtfulness that comes from caring
can accomplish more than you expect.

—*Sharon Whitley, writer*

Everybody can be great. Because anybody can serve. You don't have to have a college degree to serve. You don't have to make your subject and verb agree to serve. You don't have to know about Plato and Aristotle . . . [or] Einstein's Theory of Relativity . . . [or] the Second Theory of Thermodynamics in physics to serve. You only need a heart full of grace. A soul generated by love.

—Martin Luther King Jr., civil rights leader, clergyman, and Nobel Peace Prize winner

God appoints our graces to be
nurses to other men's weaknesses.

—Henry Ward Beecher, preacher, orator, and lecturer

❖

There is no duty more obligatory than
the repayment of kindness.

—Cicero, statesman and orator

Forget injuries, never forget kindnesses.

—*Confucius, philosopher and scholar*

❖

If I can stop one heart from breaking,
I shall not live in vain.

—*Emily Dickinson, poet*

Sometimes when we are generous in small,
barely detectable ways it can change
someone else's life forever.

—*Margaret Cho, comedian and actor*

❖

Tenderness and kindness are not signs
of weakness and despair, but manifestations
of strength and resolution.

—*Kahlil Gibran, poet and novelist*

Always be nice to people on the way up; because you'll meet the same people on the way down.

—*Wilson Mizner, writer*

❖

The everyday kindness of the back roads more than makes up for the acts of greed in the headlines.

—*Charles Kuralt, journalist*

The most important human endeavor is the striving for morality in our actions. Our inner balance and even our very existence depend on it. Only morality in our actions can give beauty and dignity to life.

—*Albert Einstein, physicist*

Kindness has converted more sinners
than zeal, eloquence or learning.

—*Frederick W. Faber, theologian and hymnist*

❖

Kindness is the golden chain by
which society is bound together.

—*Johann Wolfgang von Goethe,
writer and scientist*

This is my simple religion. There is no need for temples; no need for complicated philosophy. Our own brain, our own heart is our temple; the philosophy is kindness.

—*The Dalai Lama, religious leader*

Three things in human life are important.
The first is to be kind.
The second is to be kind.
The third is to be kind.

—*Henry James, writer*

❖

The true measure of an individual
is how he treats a person who can
do him absolutely no good.

—*Ann Landers, advice columnist*

Let us be grateful to people who make us happy; they are the charming gardeners who make our souls blossom.

—*Marcel Proust, writer*

Power is the ability to do good things for others.

—*Brooke Astor, socialite*

❖

Appreciation can make a day, even change
a life. Your willingness to put it into
words is all that is necessary.

—*Margaret Cousins, writer and editor*

Courtesies of a small and trivial character
arc the ones which strike deepest in the
grateful and appreciating heart.

—Henry Clay, statesman

❖

The good that men do lives after them.

—Ruth Gordon, actor

The true way to soften one's troubles
is to solace those of others.

—*Françoise d'Aubigne, marquise de Maintenon
(French consort of Louis XIV)*

⬥

The most exquisite pleasure is
giving pleasure to others.

—*Jean de La Bruyere, writer*

Make one person happy each day and in
forty years you will have made 14,600 human
beings happy for a little time, at least.

—*Charley Willey, writer*

❖

When you dig another out of their troubles,
you find a place to bury your own.

—*Anonymous*

To be kind to all, to like many and love a few,
to be needed and wanted by those we love, is
certainly the nearest we can come to happiness.

—*Mary Roberts Rinehart, writer*

❖

Kindness in words creates confidence.
Kindness in thinking creates profundity.
Kindness in giving creates love.

—*Lao-tzu, philosopher*

If animals could speak, the dog would be a blundering outspoken fellow; but the cat would have the rare grace of never saying a word too much.

—Mark Twain, humorist, writer, and lecturer

Kind words can be short and easy to speak but their echoes are truly endless.

—Mother Teresa, religious figure and humanitarian

Be kind, for everyone you meet
is fighting a hard battle.

—Philo, philosopher

You cannot do a kindness too soon, for you never know how soon it will be too late.

—*Ralph Waldo Emerson, essayist, poet, and philosopher*

Life is not so short but that there is always time enough for courtesy.

—*Ralph Waldo Emerson, essayist, poet, and philosopher*

Always set high value on spontaneous kindness. He whose inclination prompts him to cultivate your friendship of his own accord will love you more than one whom you have been at pains to attach to you.

—Samuel Johnson, clergyman,
philosopher, and educator

❖

If you can't be kind, at least be vague.

—Judith Martin, columnist for Miss Manners

No act of kindness, no matter how small,
is ever wasted.

—*Aesop, writer and fabulist*

❖

Being considerate of others will take your
children further in life than any college degree.

—*Marian Wright Edelman, social activist*

Remember that everyone you meet is
afraid of something, loves something
and has lost something.

—*H. Jackson Brown Jr., writer*

❖

A person who is nice to you, but rude
to the waiter, is not a nice person.

—*Dave Barry, columnist and writer*

Politeness is one half good nature
and the other half good lying.

—*Mary Wise Little, writer*

❖

See ye not, courtesy,
Is the true alchemy,
Turning to gold all it touches and tries?

—*George Meredith, writer*

Kindness is a language the dumb can speak
and the deaf can hear and understand.

—Christian Nestell Bovee, writer

Remember there's no such thing as
a small act of kindness. Every act creates
a ripple with no logical end.

—Scott Adams, cartoonist

Beginning today, treat everyone you meet as if
they were going to be dead by midnight. Extend to
them all the care, kindness and understanding you
can muster, and do it with no thought of any
reward. Your life will never be the same again.

—Og Mandino, speaker and writer

In this world, you must be a bit too kind
in order to be kind enough.

—Pierre Carlet, novelist and dramatist

⋈

Of Courtesy, it is much less than Courage of
Heart or Holiness yet in my walks it seems to
me that the Grace of God is in Courtesy.

—Hilaire Belloc, writer

The basis of all good human behavior is kindness.

—*Eleanor Roosevelt, American first lady and social activist*

❖

The greater man, the greater courtesy.

—*Alfred, Lord Tennyson, poet*

One who knows how to show and
to accept kindness will be a better
friend than any possession.

—*Sophocles, dramatist*

⬥

A part of kindness consists in loving
people more than they deserve.

—*Joseph Joubert, moralist*

Wise sayings often fall on barren ground;
but a kind word is never thrown away.

—*Sir Arthur Helps, writer*

One can pay back the loan of gold, but one lies forever in debt to those who are kind.

—Marcus Aurelius, Roman emperor

❖

I came upon a doctor who appeared in quite poor health. I said, "There's nothing that I can do for you that you can't do for yourself." He said, "Oh yes you can. Just hold my hand. I think that that would help." So I sat with him a while then I asked him how he felt. He said, "I think I'm cured."

—Conor Oberst, singer and songwriter

The keynote of American civilization is a sort of warm-hearted vulgarity. The Americans have none of the irony of the English, none of their cool poise, none of their manner. But they do have friendliness. Where an Englishman would give you his card, an American would very likely give you his shirt.

—*Raymond Chandler, writer*

Let no one ever come to you without leaving better and happier. Be the living expression of God's kindness: kindness in your face, kindness in your eyes, kindness in your smile.

—*Mother Teresa, religious figure and humanitarian*

Whoever is kind to the creatures of
God is kind to himself.

—*Muhammad, Islamic prophet*

❖

There is nothing to make you like other human
beings so much as doing things for them.

—*Zora Neale Hurston, writer*

When you carry out acts of kindness you get a wonderful feeling inside. It is as though something inside your body responds and says, yes, this is how I ought to feel.

—*Harold Kushner, rabbi and writer*

If we're really honest with ourselves, there are probably times when we think, "What possible use can I be in this world? What need is there for somebody like me to fill?" That's one of the deeper mysteries. Then God's grace comes to us in the form of another person who tells us we have been of help, and what a blessing that is.

—*Fred Rogers, television's Mister Rogers and clergyman*

If someone listens, or stretches out a hand, or whispers a kind word of encouragement, or attempts to understand a lonely person, extraordinary things begin to happen.

—*Loretta Girzartis, writer*

❖

Never underestimate the power of simple courtesy. Your courtesy may not be returned or remembered, but discourtesy will.

—*Princess Jackson Smith, writer*

The service we render others is the rent
we pay for our room on earth.

—*Wilfred Grenfell, physician and missionary*

❖

You may not have saved a lot of money in your
life, but if you have saved a lot of heartaches for
other folks, you are a pretty rich man.

—*Seth Parker, recording artist*

You don't have to be rich or famous to share
your blessings. . . . Helping others doesn't just
improve their lives; it makes you a better person.

—*Venus and Serena Williams, tennis players*

❖

A little Consideration, a little Thought
for Others, makes all the difference.

—*Eeyore to Pooh in* Winnie-The-Pooh,
A.A. Milne, writer

Whoever is happy will make others happy too.

—*Anne Frank, diarist and Holocaust victim*

❖

No one is useless in this world who lightens
the burden of it for someone else.

—*Charles Dickens, writer*

You have not lived a perfect day,
even though you have earned your money,
unless you have done something for
someone who cannot repay you.

—*Ruth Smeltzer, writer*

"Being good to people" means more than living up to conventional rules of etiquette, corporate codes of conduct, or legal requirements. It means thinking about the *other* person's point of view and treating her the way you'd want to be treated if you were in her shoes. It takes time, effort, empathy—even a bit of imagination, since it involves escaping, at least for the moment, from the little world of your own desires, needs, expectations, and entering into another person's point of view. It's no coincidence that this last tip is so close to what has come to be called The Golden Rule—"Do unto others as you would have them do unto you"—or that, in one form or another, the same principle is at the heart of all the world's great religions. There's something basic about human nature that calls upon us to live by this rule. When you follow this principle, your career is likely to thrive. At the same time, you'll be doing your part to improve the world in which you live. And that's a form of personal success that's more important and more satisfying than fame or fortune.

—Jonathan M. Tisch, chairman
and CEO of Loews Hotels

To err is human; to forgive, divine.

—*Alexander Pope, poet*

❖

Always forgive your enemies—
nothing annoys them so much.

—*Oscar Wilde, writer and wit*

Allowing an unimportant mistake to pass
without comment is a wonderful social grace.

—*Judith Martin, columnist for* Miss Manners

❖

The greatest gift you can give yourself is to
forgive. If I want to be forgiven for my mess ups
then I have to forgive everyone else when they
mess up. That's why I believe I was able to go
through cancer and I am alive today.

—*Tammy Faye Bakker-Messner, evangelist
and television personality*

It is very easy to forgive others their mistakes.
It takes more grit and gumption to forgive
them for having witnessed your own.

—*Jessamyn West, novelist*

❖

I have to forgive because I'm going
to be a bitter bitch if I don't.

—*LeAnn Rimes, country music singer*

There's no point in burying a hatchet if you're going to put up a marker on the site.

—*Sydney Harris, journalist*

❖

To forgive is the highest, most beautiful form of love. In return, you will receive untold peace and happiness.

—*Robert Muller, writer*

Life is an adventure in forgiveness.

—*Norman Cousins, editor and writer*

⬥

The weak can never forgive.
Forgiveness is the attribute of the strong.

—*Mahatma Gandhi, political leader and activist*

To forgive is to set a prisoner free
and discover the prisoner was *you*.

—*Anonymous*

I can forgive, but I cannot forget,
is only another way of saying, I will not forgive.
Forgiveness ought to be like a cancelled note—
torn in two, and burned up, so that it
never can be shown against one.

—*Henry Ward Beecher, preacher, orator, and lecturer*

There is no revenge so complete as forgiveness.

—*Josh Billings, a.k.a. Henry Wheeler Shaw, humorist*

❦

Holding on to anger, resentment,
and hurt only gives you tense muscles,
a headache and a sore jaw from clenching
your teeth. Forgiveness gives you back the
laughter and the lightness in your life.

—*Joan Lunden, television personality*

The practice of forgiveness is our most important contribution to the healing of the world.

—Marianne Williamson, writer

❖

Fear grows out of the things we think; it lives in our minds. Compassion grows out of the things we are, and lives in our hearts.

—Barbara Garrison, writer and illustrator

Perhaps we're too embarrassed to change or too frightened of the consequences of showing that we actually care. But why not risk it anyway? Begin today. Carry out a random act of seemingly senseless kindness, with no expectation or reward or punishment. Safe in the knowledge that one day, someone somewhere might do the same for you.

—*Diana, Princess of Wales*

If you help others, you will be helped, perhaps tomorrow, perhaps in one hundred years, but you will be helped. Nature must pay off the debt. . . . It is a mathematical law and all life is mathematics.

—G. I. Gurdjieff, spiritualist and writer

❖

Our lives are fed by kind words and gracious behavior. We are nourished by expression like "excuse me" and other such simple courtesies.

—Ed Hays, writer

I believe that man will not merely endure; he will prevail. He is immortal, not because he alone among the creatures has an inexhaustible voice, but because he has a soul, a spirit capable of kindness and compassion.

—*William Faulkner, writer*

❖

Courtesy is a small act but it packs a mighty wallop.

—*Anonymous*

I keep my ideals, because in spite of everything I still believe that people are really good at heart.

—*Anne Frank, diarist and Holocaust victim*

❖

If a man be gracious and courteous to strangers, it shows he is a citizen of the world, and that his heart is no island cut off from other lands, but a continent that joins to them.

—*Sir Francis Bacon, scientist, statesman, and writer*

Gratitude is the most exquisite form of courtesy.

—Jacques Maritain, philosopher

⬥

Try—and oh boy, how hard it is—to find the good in people and not the bad. . . . Nobody is perfect. Certainly not me. So *look for the good in others*. Forget the other. Clara Barton, founder and president of the Red Cross, was once reminded of a wrong a friend had done to her years earlier. "Don't you remember?" the friend asked. "No," replied Clara firmly. "I distinctly remember forgetting that." Not bad advice. Take a lesson from . . . [President George H. W. Bush]. He says when I remind him that someone has been hateful, "Isn't it better to make a friend rather than an enemy?" He's right too.

—Barbara Bush, American first lady

Any ordinary favor we do for someone or any compassionate reaching out may seem to be going nowhere at first, but may be planting a seed we can't see right now. Sometimes we need to just do the best we can and then trust in an unfolding we can't design or ordain.

—Sharon Salzberg, writer and teacher

Compassion is the basis of all morality.

—*Arthur Schopenhauer, philosopher*

❖

Compassion is a sympathetic feeling. It involves the willingness to put yourself in someone else's shoes, to take the focus off yourself and to imagine what it's like to be in someone else's predicament, and simultaneously, to feel love for that person. It's the recognition that other people's problems, their pain and frustrations, are every bit as real as our own [and are] often far worse. In recognizing this fact and trying to offer some assistance, we open our own hearts and greatly enhance our sense of gratitude.

—*Richard Carlson, medical writer and lecturer*

If you want others to be happy,
practice compassion. If you want to
be happy, practice compassion.

—*The Dalai Lama, religious leader*

❖

I know the compassion of others is a relief at
first. I don't despise it. But it can't quench pain,
it slips through your soul as through a sieve. And
when our suffering has been dragged from one
pity to another, as from one mouth to another,
we can no longer respect or love it.

—*Georges Bernano, novelist and political writer*

Compassion is an emotion of which we ought never to be ashamed. Graceful, particularly in youth, is the tear of sympathy, and the heart that melts at the tale of woe. We should not permit ease and indulgence to contract our affections, and wrap us up in a selfish enjoyment; but we should accustom ourselves to think of the distresses of human life, of the solitary cottage; the dying parent, and the weeping orphan. Nor ought we ever to sport with pain and distress in any of our amusements, or treat even the meanest insect with wanton cruelty.

—*Hugh Blair, clergyman, critic, and professor of rhetoric and belles lettres*

Until he extends his circle of compassion to all living things, man will not find peace.

—*Albert Schweitzer, theologian, musician, and medical missionary*

❖

I ain't no saint, but I've tried never to do anything that would hurt my family or offend God. . . . I figure all any kid needs is hope and the feeling he or she belongs. If I could do or say anything that would give some kid that feeling, I would believe I had contributed something to the world.

—*Elvis Presley, singer*

What do we live for if not to make
life less difficult for each other?

—George Eliot, writer
(born as Mary Ann Evans)

When a man has compassion for others,
God has compassion for him.

—*Talmud*

⬦

The measure of love is compassion;
the measure of compassion is kindness.

—*St. Paul, Apostle*

The value of compassion cannot be over-emphasized. Anyone can criticize. It takes a true believer to be compassionate. No greater burden can be borne by an individual than to know no one cares or understands.

—*Arthur H. Stainback, educator and writer*

Compassion brings us to a stop, and for a moment we rise above ourselves.

—*Mason Cooley, aphorist*

Dogs seem to understand what we don't: that we should surround ourselves with people who are a "net positive" in our lives—people who bring us (and to whom we can bring), on the whole, more happiness, more fun, more learning, more love. In short, those who make us better people. For such people, we need to be more accepting and more forgiving, and there is no excuse for holding a grudge. Even the best of people will make little mistakes, be a little selfish, be a little insensitive. In the great scheme of life, these are small things, and we should let them pass over us, and always run back and make friends, no matter who was "at fault." And in the spirit of friendship, or when we feel that we do need to say something about these little slights to clear the air, dogs once again can provide a good lesson: never bite when a simple growl will do.

—W. R. Pursche, *writer*

form

Grace also reveals itself through form—poise, style, manners, and bearing. Have you heard someone say they plan to grow old gracefully? Do you know anyone who always seemed to have a little more class than their peers, and it doesn't always have to do with how he or she is dressed? Think of the late Princess Grace of Monaco—didn't her name suit her perfectly?

When a person expends the least amount
of motion on one action, that is grace.

—Anton Pavlovich Chekhov,
writer and playwright

Grace was in all her steps,
Heaven in her eye.

—John Milton, poet

⌖

A woman of such uncommon
grace has no need of guile.

—Henry James, writer

[Scarlett O'Hara's mother, Ellen] was
a tall woman, standing a head higher than
her fiery husband, but she moved with such
quiet grace in her swaying hoops that her
height attracted no attention to itself. . . .
She quickly brought order, dignity and
grace into Gerald's household and she gave
to Tara a beauty it had never had before.

—*Margaret Mitchell, writer,* Gone with the Wind

❖

The test of good manners is to be able
to put up pleasantly with bad ones.

—*Wendell L. Willkie, American politician
and presidential nominee*

Grace is in garments, in movements, in manners; beauty in the nude, and in forms. This is true of bodies; but when we speak of feelings, beauty is in their spirituality, and grace in their moderation.

—Joseph Joubert, *moralist*

Good breeding consists in concealing
how much we think of ourselves and how
little we think of the other person.

—*Mark Twain, humorist, writer, and lecturer*

✦

I place a high moral value on the way people
behave. I find it repellent to have a lot, and to
behave with anything other than courtesy
in the old sense of the word—politeness of the
heart, a gentleness of the spirit.

—*Fran Lebowitz, writer and humorist*

It's a sign of mediocrity when you
demonstrate gratitude with moderation.

—*Roberto Benigni, actor and director*

And yet—it is not beauty that inspires
the deepest passion. Beauty without grace
is the hook without the bait. Beauty,
without expression, tires.

—*Ralph Waldo Emerson, essayist,
poet, and philosopher*

❖

Tact is, after all, a kind of mind reading.

—*Sara Orne Jewett, writer*

Good manners sometimes means simply
putting up with other people's bad manners.

—*H. Jackson Brown Jr., writer*

❖

We should give as we would receive, cheerfully,
quickly, and without hesitation; for there is no
grace in a benefit that sticks to the fingers.

—Seneca, *philosopher, statesman, and tutor of Nero*

Ben Bradlee wrote a book about President Kennedy after he died, and it was called *That Special Grace*. J. F. K. Jr. had it too, though history didn't give him wars and great movements in which to show it. But he showed it anyway. Not so long ago, the day his mother was buried, after the prayers and the graveside service at Arlington, when everyone was starting to leave, young John Kennedy stepped up to the casket of his mother and the gravestone of his father. He leaned forward and stretched toward them and put his hand upon each with a touch that was more like a kiss. It was an act of great physical grace, and love, and maybe it was done in part on behalf of a country that felt as he did—a generous gesture like the one thirty years before when a little boy made a salute.

—*Peggy Noonan, speechwriter, writer, and commentator*

One of the few graces of getting old—and God knows there are few graces—is that if you've worked hard and kept your nose to the grindstone, something happens: The body gets old but the creative mechanism is refreshed, smoothed and oiled and honed. That is the grace. That is what's happening to me.

—Maurice Sendak, *children's writer and illustrator*

Clothes and manners do not make
the man; but when he is made, they
greatly improve his appearance.

—*Arthur Ashe, tennis player and activist*

❖

When grace is joined with wrinkles,
it is adorable. There is an unspeakable
dawn in happy old age.

—*Victor Hugo, writer*

Old age is no such uncomfortable thing,
if one gives oneself up to it with a good grace,
and don't drag it about to midnight dances
and the public show.

—Horace Walpole, writer and historian

❖

I don't plan to grow old gracefully. I plan
to have face-lifts until my ears meet.

—Rita Rudner, comedian and writer

Youth, large, lusty, loving—
youth full of grace, force, fascination.
Do you know that Old Age may come after
you with equal grace, force, fascination?

—*Walt Whitman, poet*

It's nothing to be born ugly. Sensibly,
the ugly woman comes to terms with her
ugliness and exploits it as a grace of nature.
To become ugly means the beginning of a
calamity, self-willed most of the time.

—*Colette [Sidonie Gabrielle Colette], writer*

⬥

Nothing is harder to do gracefully
than getting off your high horse.

—*Anonymous*

Never start an argument
unless you are well dressed.

—*Anonymous*

❖

And footsteps! I can't stand the vulgarity
of a woman who makes a noise when she
walks. It's all right for soldiers, but when
I was growing up the quintessence of
breeding in a lady was a quiet footstep.

—*Diana Vreeland, former editor in chief
of* Vogue *magazine*

I seek constantly to improve my
manners and graces, for they are the
sugar to which all are attracted.

—*Og Mandino, motivational
speaker and writer*

Do not be the last to leave the ballroom.
It is more elegant to leave early, as staying
too late gives others the impression that you
do not often have an invitation to a ball,
and must make the most of it.

—*Cecil B. Hartley, writer*

⟡

It's not the correct thing to put the
spoon or fork so far into the mouth
that the bystanders are doubtful
of its return to the light.

—*The Correct Thing in Good Society*

Can't Christians be sexy too? Why not? Just because you ask Jesus in your life doesn't mean you're not a girl or a woman. Christians love sex and I love to be sexy. If I walked around in an old ratty dress, without my hair done and no make-up, I could have preached all day long and nobody would want what I had. Instead, they would say, "Brother, if I have to look like that, forget about it!" But when they found out that you could wear make-up and you can be sexy and have a lot of fun, the Gospel was more palatable to them because they realized that you don't have to give up everything. You don't have to give up fun to serve God.

—*Tammy Faye Bakker-Messner, evangelist and television personality*

JOB INTERVIEWER: Not many people have grace.

ELAINE: Well, you know, grace is a tough one.
I like to think I have a little grace.
Not as much as Jackie O . . .

INTERVIEWER: You can't have a *little* grace.
You either have grace or you don't.

ELAINE: Okay, fine. I have no grace.

INTERVIEWER: And you can't acquire grace.

ELAINE: Well, I have no intention of
getting grace.

INTERVIEWER: Grace isn't something you
can pick up at the market.

ELAINE: All right, all right, look,
I don't *have* grace, I don't *want* grace,
I don't even *say* grace, okay?

INTERVIEWER: Thank you for coming in.

ELAINE: Yeah yeah right.

—Larry David, Bill Masters, and Bob Shaw,
writers for the television sitcom Seinfeld

Oh, never mind the fashion.
When one has a style of one's own,
it is always twenty times better.

—*Margaret Oliphant, writer*

❖

Sensible women do not accept the moving
pictures as an index to style. The actress may be
wearing gowns that are beautiful, effective, but
they may not be in good taste.

—*Lillian Eichler, writer,* The New Book of
Etiquette, *vol. 2,* 1924 Form

I have always dressed according to certain
Basic Guy Fashion Rules, Including: Both of
your socks should always be the same color,
Or they should at least both be fairly dark.

—*Dave Barry, columnist and writer*

❖

DEAR MISS MANNERS: Some time ago, a
lady was dancing with her male friend at the
White House and her underslip dropped off on
the dance floor, and the lady just kept dancing
as if nothing had happened. Was this the
proper thing for the lady to do?

GENTLE READER: Yes, the thing to do is to
ignore it. A general rule of etiquette is that
one apologizes for the unfortunate occurrence,
but the unthinkable is unmentionable.

—*Judith Martin, columnist for* Miss Manners

It is correct to remember that a woman
who is pinched in at the waist with tight
corsets, throttled around the neck with a tight
collar, and cramped as to her feet with tight,
high-heeled shoes, will walk about as
gracefully as a swan on a turnpike road.

—*Florence Howe Hall, writer*

❖

Dance with grace and modesty, neither affect to
make a parade of your knowledge; refrain from
great leaps and ridiculous jumps, which would
attract the attention of all towards you.

—*Anonymous*

Elegance is not the prerogative of those who have just escaped from adolescence, but of those who have already taken possession of their future.

—Coco Chanel, fashion designer

In life as in the dance:
Grace glides on blistered feet.

—Alice Abrams, writer

Certain daring necklines have a paralyzing
effect on the conversation and even on the
appetite of the other dinner party guests, who
hope to see a little more than is already revealed
and would love to change places with the waiter,
who has a particularly stimulating view.

—*Genevieve Antoine Dariaux, writer,*
Accent on Elegance

Today, fashion is really about sensuality—
how a woman feels on the inside. In the eighties
women used suits with exaggerated shoulders and
waists to make a strong impression. Women are
now more comfortable with themselves and their
bodies—they no longer feel the need to
hide behind their clothes.

—*Donna Karan, fashion designer*

Today you see Julia Roberts and Cameron Diaz running around looking unkempt in jogging trousers. They look like bag ladies, like homeless people. In the past, actresses had to commit in their contracts to appear in public like stars when they left their homes.

—Valentino, haute couture designer

❧

If I were wearing a tuxedo I'd want to wear it with satin Converse sneakers. I'd want my tuxedo to be shrunken and ill-fitting, so I'd look like one of the John Holmstrom cartoons from *Punk* magazine. It's the idea of imperfection, of being awkward.

—Marc Jacobs, fashion designer

Few men of action have been able to
make a graceful exit at the appropriate time.

—Malcolm Muggeridge, journalist,
writer, and media personality

Delicacy is to love what grace is to beauty.

—*Françoise d'Aubigne, marquise de Maintenon*
(French consort of Louis XIV)

❖

Severe plainness is always elegant.

—*Annina Periam Danton, writer,*
Western Etiquette

What's a fine person, or a beauteous face,

Unless deportment gives them decent grace?

Blessed with all other requisites to please,

Some want the striking elegance of ease;

The curious eye their awkward movement tires:

They seem like puppets let about by wires.

—*Charles Churchill, poet and essayist*

❖

Miss Ruth was a lady.

And a lady always knows when to leave.

—*Fannie Flagg, writer, from* Fried Green Tomatoes

action

Grace in action doesn't necessarily mean physical movement. This type of grace reveals itself in everyday acts. The writer Ernest Hemingway summed it up best when he coined the phrase "Grace under pressure," meaning to act with poise and dignity even in the worst of situations. Acts of grace often require contemplation, humility, patience, insight, and even humor.

Grace under pressure.

—Ernest Hemingway, writer (Ernest Hemingway's
definition of "guts," taken from the Latin motto
"fortiter in re, suaviter in modo")

❖

But I want first of all—in fact as an end to
these other desires—to be at peace with myself.
I want a singleness of eye, a purity of intention,
a central core to my life that will enable me
to carry out these obligations and activities as
well as I can. I want in fact—to borrow from
the language of the saints—to live "in grace" as
much of the time as possible. I am not using this
term in a strictly theological sense. By grace I
mean an inner harmony, essentially spiritual,
which can be translated into outward harmony.

—Anne Morrow Lindbergh, writer and
wife of Charles A. Lindbergh

Like any other gift, the gift of grace can be yours only if you'll reach out and take it. Maybe being able to reach out and take it is a gift, too.

—*Anonymous*

From what we get, we can make a living.
What we give, however, makes a life.

—*Arthur Ashe, tennis player, AIDS spokesperson,*
and author of Days of Grace

❖

Humor is not a trick, not jokes.
Humor is a presence in the world—
like grace—and shines on everybody.

—*Garrison Keillor, humorist, singer,*
storyteller, writer, and radio show host
of Prairie Home Companion

Do you know that the ready concession of minor points is a part of the grace of life?

—*Henry Harland, novelist*

High station in life is earned by the gallantry with which appalling experiences are survived with grace.

—*Tennessee Williams, playwright*

Everything that slows us down and
forces patience, everything that sets us
back into the slow circles of nature, is a help.
Gardening is an instrument of grace.

—*May Sarton, poet and novelist*

❖

What do I want to take home from my summer
vacation? Time. The wonderful luxury of being
at rest. The days when you shut down the mental
machinery that keeps life on track and let life
simply wander. The days when you stop
planning, analyzing, thinking and just are.
Summer is my period of grace.

—*Ellen Goodman, journalist*

As in nature. And in the arts, so in grace; it is rough treatment that gives souls as well as stones, their lustre. The more the diamond is cut the brighter it sparkles, and in what seems hard dealing God has no end in view but to perfect our graces. He sends tribulations, but tells us their purpose, that tribulation worketh patience, and patience experience, and experience hope.

—Thomas Guthrie, clergyman and philanthropist

❖

When you begin to touch your heart or let your heart be touched, you begin to discover that it's bottomless, that it doesn't have any resolution, that this heart is huge, vast, and limitless. You begin to discover how much warmth and gentleness is there, as well as how much space.

—Pema Chodron, Buddhist nun

You say grace before meals. All right. But I say grace before the concert and the opera, and grace before the play and pantomime, and grace before I open a book, and grace before sketching, painting, swimming, fencing, boxing, walking, playing, dancing, and grace before I dip the pen in the ink.

—G. K. Chesterton, writer

We who lived in concentration camps can remember the men who walked through the huts comforting others, giving away their last piece of bread. They may have been few in number, but they offer sufficient proof that everything can be taken from a man but one thing: the last of the human freedoms—to choose one's attitude in any given set of circumstances, to choose one's own way.

—*Viktor Frankl, neurologist, psychiatrist, and Holocaust survivor*

In a moment of grace, we can grasp eternity in the palm of our hand. This is the *gift* given to *creative* individuals who can identify with the *mysteries* of *life* through *art.*

—*Marcel Marceau, mime*

Within *sorrow* is grace. When we come close to those things that break us down, we touch those things that also break us open. And in that breaking open, we uncover our true *nature*.

—*Wayne Muller, writer*

❖

Too often we underestimate the power of a touch, a smile, a kind word, a listening ear, an honest compliment, or the smallest act of caring, all of which have the potential to turn a life around.

—*Leo Buscaglia, inspirational writer*

During my second year of nursing school our professor gave us a quiz. I breezed through the questions until I read the last one: "What is the first name of the woman who cleans the school?" Surely this was a joke. I had seen the cleaning woman several times, but how would I know her name? I handed in my paper, leaving the last question blank. Before the class ended, one student asked if the last question would count toward our grade. "Absolutely," the professor said. "In your careers, you will meet many people. All are significant. They deserve your attention and care, even if all you do is smile and say hello." I've never forgotten that lesson. I also learned her name was Dorothy.

—Joann C. Jones, writer and nurse

Difficulty need not foreshadow despair or defeat.
Rather achievement can be all the more
satisfying because of obstacles surmounted.

—*William Hastie, judge and politician*

❖

Make it a practice to judge persons and
things in the most favorable light at all
times and under all circumstances.

—*St. Vincent de Paul, priest*

I have seen manners that make a similar impression with personal beauty; that give the like exhilaration, and refine us like that; and, in memorable experiences, they are suddenly better than beauty, and make that superfluous and ugly. But they must be marked by fine perception, the acquaintance with real beauty. They must always show self-control: you shall not be facile, apologetic, or leaky, but king over your word; and every gesture and action shall indicate power at rest. Then they must be inspired by the good heart. There is no beautifier of complexion, or form, or behavior, like the wish to scatter joy and not pain around us. 'Tis good to give a stranger a meal, or a night's lodging. 'Tis better to be hospitable to his good meaning and thought, and give courage to a companion. We must be as courteous to a man as we are to a picture, which we are willing to give the advantage of a good light.

—*Ralph Waldo Emerson,*
essayist, poet, and philosopher

Life isn't about winning everything, it's about having the grace to learn about yourself and, by putting yourself against the challenges of sport, you don't only learn about sporting techniques but you also learn about what sort of person you are, what kind of character you are.

—*Lynn Davies, Olympic gold medalist*

⬥

Handle conflict with grace when you're boiling inside, never let others see you come unglued. People will be receptive to working with you if you can maintain a calm, unwavering demeanor in the best and worst of situations.

—*Jacqueline Whitmore, international etiquette expert*

Get a life in which you are generous. Look around at the azaleas and making fuchsia star bursts in spring; look at a full moon hanging silver in a black sky on a cold night. And realize that life is glorious, and that you have no business taking it for granted. Care so deeply about its goodness that you want to spread it around. Take the money you would have spent on beers in a bar and give it to charity. Work in a soup kitchen. Tutor a seventh-grader. All of us want to do well. But if we do not do good, too, then doing well will never be enough.

—Anna Quindlen, writer

It was really overwhelming to see the way that people responded—the kind of class and grace, and compassion and support, and resourcefulness that people showed. It was almost like rather than knocking us down, Sept. 11 kind of stepped us up. I was very impressed with that. It showed me that there's really nothing we can't handle.

—*Liev Schreiber, actor*

The hardest job kids face today is learning good manners without seeing any.

—*Fred Astaire, dancer and actor*

The maelstrom of fatherhood is a chance to show grace under real pressure, to be cool despite the chaos of your son's room. That's something that's worth a fellow's time.

—*Hugh O'Neill, writer*

What a gift of grace to be able to take the chaos from within and from it create some semblance of order.

—*Katherine Paterson, children's writer*

To finish a work? To finish a picture?
What nonsense! To finish it means to be
through with it, to kill it, to rid it of its soul, to
give it its final blow the coup de grace for the
painter as well as for the picture.

—*Pablo Picasso, artist*

❖

Part of the difficulty of all this is that you
write for an audience who doesn't know what
grace is and don't recognize it when they see it.
All my stories are about the action of grace
on a character who is not very willing to support
it, but most people think of these stories
as hard, hopeless, brutal, etc.

—*Flannery O'Connor, writer*

I still when I wake up hit the ground running;
and having an illness, I'm only one of hundreds
of thousands of people that live with an illness,
and I'm just in awe of the bravery and dignity
of the people I see at the hospital.

—Karen Duffy, former model and actor

❖

I wanted a perfect ending. Now I've learned,
the hard way, that some poems don't rhyme,
and some stories don't have a clear beginning,
middle, and end. Life is about not knowing,
having to change, taking the moment and
making the best of it without knowing
what's going to happen next.

—Gilda Radner, actor

redemption

Perhaps the greatest grace is redemption—to be forgiven, wholly and completely. Every one of us falls from grace from time to time. We're all prey to anger, grudges, deception, and other weaknesses. Through the grace of God, the grace of others, and the grace within our own hearts, honor, faith, and dignity are restored.

Grace me no grace, nor uncle me no uncle;
I am no traitor's uncle, and that word "grace"
In an ungracious mouth is but profane.

—*William Shakespeare, dramatist and poet*

⟡

Whoever strives to withdraw from
obedience, withdraws from grace.

—*Thomas à Kempis, monk and writer*

To hit bottom is to fall from grace.

—Doug Horton, writer

❖

He who forgiveth, and is reconciled unto
his enemy, shall receive his reward from God;
for he loveth not the unjust doers.

—The Koran

Anger makes you smaller, while forgiveness forces you to grow beyond what you were.

—Cherie Carter-Scott, inspirational writer

We all like to forgive, and love best not those who offend us least, nor who have done most for us, but those who make it most easy for us to forgive them.

—*Samuel Butler, writer*

❦

Once a woman has forgiven her man, she must not reheat his sins for breakfast.

—*Marlene Dietrich, actor*

The best way to knock the chip off your neighbor's shoulder is to pat him on the back.

—*Anonymous*

❖

I know that there are people who do not love their fellow man, and I hate people like that!

—*Tom Lehrer, mathematician and humorist*

In the Bible it says they asked Jesus how many times you should forgive, and he said seventy times seven. Well, I want you all to know that I'm keeping a chart.

—*Hillary Rodham Clinton, U.S. Senator*

The opposite of sin is grace, not virtue.

—*Philip Yancey, writer*

❖

Hell is yourself and the only redemption
is when a person puts himself aside to
feel deeply for another person.

—*Tennessee Williams, writer*

The salvation of this human world lies
nowhere else than in the human heart,
in the human power to reflect, in human
meekness and human responsibility.

—*Vaclav Havel, poet*

❖

Rudeness is the weak man's
imitation of strength.

—*Eric Hoffer, writer*

As long as you don't forgive, who and whatever it is will occupy rent-free space in your mind.

—Isabelle Holland, *writer*

Don't carry a grudge. While you're carrying the grudge, the other guy's out dancing.

—*Buddy Hackett, comedian and actor*

❖

Surely it is much more generous to forgive and remember, than to forgive and forget.

—*Maria Edgeworth, novelist*

No, I'm through with everything here.
I want peace. I want to see if somewhere
there isn't something left in life of charm and
grace. Do you know what I'm talking about?

—*Rhett Butler in* Gone with the Wind,
Margaret Mitchell, writer

⬦

Storms make trees take deeper roots.

—*Dolly Parton, singer and songwriter*

Accept that at times you will get in the way of your brothers—thus becoming a cross to bear, and thus becoming grace.

—*Madeleine Delbrel, writer*

There's a trick to the Graceful Exit. It begins with the vision to recognize when a job, a life stage, a relationship is over—and to let go. It means leaving what's over without denying its value.

—*Ellen Goodman, journalist*

outlook

Everyone has his or her own philosophy
about how to live. Let grace guide your
personal outlook on life. You'll see that
grace touches on everything—including how
to love, accept humility, create beauty,
forgive others, and endure hardship.
In short, grace teaches us how to live.

Life. . . . It tends to respond to our outlook,
to shape itself to meet our expectations.

—*Richard M. DeVos, founder of Amway Corp.*

❖

Grace is always natural, though that does not
prevent its being often used to hide a lie.

—*Marquis de Custine, writer*

God, give us grace to accept with serenity the things that cannot be changed, courage to change the things which should be changed and the wisdom to distinguish the one from the other.

—ORIGINALLY PART OF A SERMON IN 1943 AND LATER USED BY ALCOHOLICS ANONYMOUS, QUOTED BY REINHOLD NIEBUHR, THEOLOGIAN

Love that goes upward is worship. Love that goes outward is affection. Love that stoops is grace.

—*Donald Grey Barnhouse, pastor and biblical scholar*

Verily, great grace may go with a little gift; and precious are all things that come from friends.

—*Theocritus, poet*

There will always be someone else with a different view than you. I appreciate them and would never say that they are wrong. I hope that they would give me that courtesy also.

—*Melissa Etheridge, singer*

❖

It is not in virtue of its liberty that the human will attains to grace, it is much rather by grace that it attains to liberty.

—*St. Augustine, theologian*

Responsibility does not only lie with the leaders of our countries or with those who have been appointed or elected to do a particular job. It lies with each of us individually. Peace, for example, starts within each one of us. When we have inner peace, we can be at peace with those around us.

—*The Dalai Lama, religious leader*

Whining is not only graceless,
but can be dangerous. It can alert a brute
that a victim is in the neighborhood.

—Maya Angelou, poet and actor

⬥

Unearned gifts and unexpected
pleasures bring the most joy.

—Philip Yancey, writer

I absolutely do not regret the jewels I sold. I've only got one pair of ears and one neck. And the sale has enabled me to live a more balanced life.

—*Princess Salimah Aga Khan, activist and former wife of Aga Khan*

❖

If you see a whole thing—it seems that it's always beautiful. Planets, lives. . . . But up close a world's all dirt and rocks. And day to day, life's a hard job, you get tired, you lose the pattern.

—*Ursula K. Le Guin, writer*

Rather than fight their feelings and panic simply because they are feeling bad, they accept their feelings. Knowing that this too shall pass. Rather than stumbling and fighting against their negative feelings, they are graceful in their acceptance of them. This allows them to come gently and gracefully out of negative feeling states into more positive states of mind. One of the happiest people I know is someone who also gets quite low from time to time. The difference, it seems, is that he has become comfortable with his low moods. It's almost as though he doesn't really care because he knows that in due time, he will be happy again. To him, it's no big deal.

—*Richard Carlson,*
medical writer and lecturer

There is one purpose to life and one only:
to bear witness to and understand as much
as possible of the complexity of the world—
its beauty, its mysteries, its riddles. The more
you understand, the more you look, the
greater is your enjoyment of life and your
sense of peace. That's all there is to it. If an
activity is not grounded in "to love" or
"to learn," it does not have value.

—*Ellen Goodman, journalist*

No man or woman of the humblest sort
can really be strong, gentle, and good, without
the world being better for it, without somebody
being helped and comforted by the very
existence of that goodness.

—*Alan Alda, actor*

If there's a child on the South Side of Chicago who can't read, that matters to me, even if it's not my child. If there's a senior citizen who can't pay for their prescription drugs and has to choose between medicine and the rent, that makes my life poorer, even if it's not my grandparent. If there's an Arab American family being rounded up without benefit of an attorney or due process, that threatens my civil liberties.

—*Barak Obama, politician*

An authentic prophet is one who prophesies in fashion that does not comfort people, but actually calls them to make some new sacrifices. That's an authentic prophet, whether one speaks in the name of God or whatever. A great deal of authentic prophetism in the modern world is to be found in nonreligious terms and in nonchurch configurations, often even hostile to the church. The churches themselves have broadly failed in the prophetic function. Therefore a good deal of so-called atheism is itself, from my point of view, theologically significant. It is the working of God in history, and judgment upon the pious. An authentic prophet can and should be a radical critic of spurious piety, of sham spirituality.

—*James Luther Adams, theologian*

I distrust those people who know so well
what God wants them to do because I notice
it always coincides with their own desires.

—*Susan B. Anthony, suffragist and writer*

❖

Anywhere I see suffering, that is where
I want to be, doing what I can.

—*Diana, Princess of Wales*

A singer starts by having his instrument
as a gift from God. . . . When you have been
given something in a moment of grace,
it is sacrilegious to be greedy.

—*Marian Anderson, singer*

I grew up in the '40s and I heard all these great speeches, like Winston Churchill. His most famous, or infamous commencement exercise speech was one that consisted of seven words. He stood before this graduating class and said: "Never, never, never, never, never give up."

— *Johnny Cash, country singer and songwriter*

❖

The general outlook is not that the person has died but that the person has lived.

— *William Buchanan, businessman and philanthropist*

Your outlook upon life, your estimate of yourself, your estimate of your value are largely colored by your environment. Your whole career will be modified, shaped, molded by your surroundings, by the character of the people with whom you come in contact every day.

—*Orison Swett Marden, author and founder of* Success *magazine*

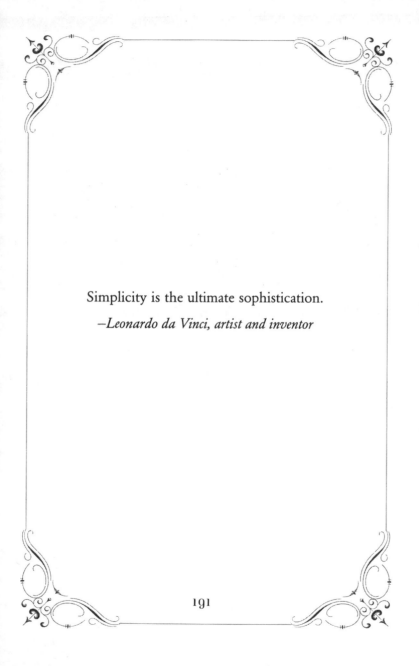

Simplicity is the ultimate sophistication.

—Leonardo da Vinci, artist and inventor

selected sources

WHAT IS GRACE?

Gulley, Philip and James, Mulholland, *If God is Love—Rediscovering Grace in an Ungracious World.* San Francisco: Harper, 2004.

Lamott: "The Grace of Klutz" By Anne Lamott. *Salon.com,* December, 1997.

SOUL

Lamott: *Traveling Mercies: Some Thoughts on Faith,* Pantheon/Anchor, 1999/2000.

HEART

Sullivan, Andrew: "When Grace Arrives Unannounced," *Time* Magazine. March 28, 2005.

Rogers: Rogers, Fred. *The World According to Mister Rogers: Important Things to Remember.* Hyperion, 2003.

Williams: Venus and Serena Williams: *Serving from the Hip: 10 Rules for Living, Loving and Winning.* Houghton Mifflin, 2005.

Tisch: Tisch, Jonathan M. with Karl Weber: *The Power of We—Succeeding Through Partnerships,* John Wiley & Sons, 2004.

Bush: Bush, Barbara: *A Memoir.* Guideposts, 1994.

Pursche: Pursche, W.R.: *The Canine Commandments: Lessons to Live By.* Varzara House, 2005.

FORM

Noonan, Peggy: John Fitzgerald Kennedy, Jr., "Grace Under the Glare," *Time* Magazine. July 26, 1999.

ACTION

Lindbergh: Lindbergh, Anne Morrow: *Gift from the Sea.* New York, Pantheon, 1955, 1975.

Quindlen: Quindlen, Anna: *A Short Guide to a Happy Life.* New York, Random House, 2000.

Radner: Radner, Gilda: *It's Always Something.* New York, Simon and Schuster, 1989.

REDEMPTION

Yancey: Yancey, Philip: *What's So Amazing About Grace?* Grand Rapids, Zondervan, 1992.

Delbrel: Delbrel, Madeleine: *The Little Monk – Wisdom from a Little Friend of Big Faith.* Crossroad Publishing, 2005.

OUTLOOK

Angelou: Angelou, Maya: *I Know Why the Caged Bird Sings.* New York, Bantam, 1983.

Carlson: Carlson, Richard: *Don't Sweat the Small Stuff,* Hyperion, 1997.

Obama: Obama, Barak: *Dreams From My Father: A Story of Race and Inheritance.* New York, Three Rivers Press, 2004.

permissions

speaker list

32. Thich Nhat Hanh
33. Carolyn Hobbs
34. Tom Cruise
35. Sogyal Rinpoche
36. Carl G. Jung
37. Kathie Lee Gifford
38. Elizabeth Barrett Browning
39. Goldie Hawn
40. Norman Fitzroy Maclean
41. Billy Graham

HEART

1. J.M. Barrie
2. Eric Hoffer
3. Publius Syrus
4. Talmud
5. Andrew Sullivan
6. Mark Twain
7. Arnold Glasow
8. Sharon Whitley
9. Martin Luther King, Jr.
10. Henry Ward Beecher
11. Cicero
12. Confucius
13. Emily Dickinson
14. Margaret Cho
15. Kahlil Gibran
16. Wilson Mizner
17. Charles Kuralt
18. Albert Einstein
19. Frederick W. Faber
20. Johann Wolfgang von Goethe
21. The Dalai Lama
22. Henry James
23. Ann Landers
24. Marcel Proust
25. Brooke Astor
26. Margaret Cousins
27. Henry Clay
28. Ruth Gordon
29. Francoise d'Aubigne
30. Jean de La Bruyere
31. Charley Willey
32. Mary Roberts Rinehart
33. Lao-tzu
34. Mark Twain
35. Mother Teresa
36. Philo
37. Ralph Waldo Emerson
38. Samuel Johnson
39. Judith Martin [Miss Manners]
40. Aesop
41. Marian Wright Edelman
42. H. Jackson Brown

43. Dave Barry
44. Mary Wise Little
45. George Meredith
46. Christian Nestell Bovee
47. Scott Adams
48. Og Mandino
49. Pierre Carlet
50. Hilaire Belloc
51. Eleanor Roosevelt
52. Alfred, Lord Tennyson
53. Sophocles
54. Joseph Joubert
55. Sir Arthur Helps
56. Marcus Aurelius
57. Conor Oberst
58. Raymond Chandler
59. Mother Teresa
60. Muhammad
61. Zora Neale Hurston
62. Harold Kushner
63. Fred Rogers
64. Loretta Girzartis
65. Princess Jackson Smith
66. Wilfred Grenfell
67. Seth Parker
68. Venus and Serena Williams
69. A.A. Milne
70. Anne Frank
71. Charles Dickens

72. Ruth Smeltzer
73. Jonathan M. Tisch
74. Alexander Pope
75. Oscar Wilde
76. Judith Martin [Miss Manners]
77. Tammy Faye Bakker-Messner
78. Jessamyn West
79. LeAnn Rimes
80. Sydney Harris
81. Robert Muller
82. Norman Cousins
83. Mahatma Gandhi
84. Henry Ward Beecher
85. Josh Billings aka Henry Wheeler Shaw
86. Joan Lunden
87. Marianne Williamson
88. Barbara Garrison
89. Diana, Princess of Wales
90. G.I. Gurdjieff
91. Ed Hays
92. William Faulkner
93. Anne Frank
94. Sir Francis Bacon
95. Jacques Maritain
96. Barbara Bush
97. Sharon Salzberg

98. Arthur Schopenhauer
99. Richard Carlson
100. The Dalai Lama
101. Georges Bernano
102. Hugh Blair
103. Albert Schweitzer
104. Elvis Presley
105. George Eliot
106. The Talmud
107. St. Paul
108. Arthur H. Stainback
109. Mason Cooley
110. W.R. Pursche

FORM

1. Anton Pavlovich Chekhov
2. John Milton
3. Henry James
4. Margaret Mitchell
5. Wendell L. Willkie
6. Joseph Joubert
7. Mark Twain
8. Fran Lebowitz
9. Roberto Benigni
10. Ralph Waldo Emerson
11. Sara Orne Jewett
12. H. Jackson Brown, Jr.

13. Seneca
14. Peggy Noonan
15. Maurice Sendak
16. Arthur Ashe
17. Victor Hugo
18. Horace Walpole
19. Rita Rudner
20. Walt Whitman
21. Colette
22. Diana Vreeland
23. Og Mandino
24. Cecil B. Hartley
25. Tammy Faye Bakker-
    Messner
26. Larry David
    Bill Masters
    Bob Shaw
27. Margaret Oliphant
28. Lillian Eichler
29. David Barry
30. Judith Martin [Miss
    Manners]
31. Florence Howe Hall
32. Coco Chanel
33. Alice Abrams
34. Genevieve Antoine
    Dariaux
35. Donna Karan
36. Valentino

37. Marc Jacobs
38. Malcolm Muggeridge
39. Francoise d'Aubigne
40. Annina Periam Danton
41. Charles Churchill
42. Fannie Flagg

ACTION

1. Ernest Hemingway
2. Anne Morrow Lindbergh
3. Arthur Ashe
4. Garrison Keillor
5. Henry Harland
6. Tennessee Williams
7. May Sarton
8. Ellen Goodman
9. Thomas Guthrie
10. Pema Chodron
11. G.K. Chesterton
12. Viktor Frankl
13. Marcel Marceau
14. Wayne Muller
15. Leo Buscaglia
16. Joann C. Jones
17. William Hastie
18. St. Vincent de Paul
19. Ralph Waldo Emerson

20. Lynn Davies
21. Jacqueline Whitmore
22. Anna Quindlen
23. Live Schreiber
24. Fred Astaire
25. Hugh O'Neill
26. Katherine Paterson
27. Pablo Picasso
28. Flannery O'Connor
29. Karen Duffy
30. Gilda Radner

REDEMPTION

1. William Shakespeare
2. Thomas a Kempis
3. Doug Horton
4. The Koran
5. Cherie Carter-Scott
6. Samuel Butler
7. Marlene Dietrich
8. Tom Lehrer
9. Hillary Rodham Clinton
10. Philip Yancey
11. Tennessee Williams
12. Vaclav Havel
13. Eric Hoffer
14. Isabelle Holland

OUTLOOK

acknowledgments

If it were not for the following people, this book would not have come about and I am so grateful to each and every one. First and foremost, I thank my Random House Publisher, and more importantly, my life-long friend, Sheryl Stebbins, who asked if I'd be interested in gathering "just a few quotes" on the concept of *Grace*. I also send a huge thank you to my editor, Jena Pincott, also known as "Command Central," whose help, support, and expertise made this book what it is. Jena, you truly do have the gift and I am grateful you have shared it with me and our readers. Thank you also to Kelly Corona, whose long hours of incredible research are most appreciated. To my friends who contributed ideas, quotes and encouragement: Bob Koehler, Penny Lyon, Sue Driver, Libby Sukarochana, and Larry Brehl, thank you so much. A big thank you goes to my friend, Darlene Loebig. Dar, your input was greater than you know. With your vast wisdom, broad shoulders and infinite patience, I couldn't have had a better guide through this adventure. Many thanks go to Diane Gloor and Roberta Eckman in the Volunteer Office of UPMC/Passavant Hospital, as well as to my fellow volunteers who graciously rearranged their schedules so I could have the time to work on this book. I also thank the staff of the hospital's Outpatient Surgery Department for showing me grace every day. There's no greater care—anywhere. To my dear friend, Barb Wyllie for your love and encouragement, what I would do without you? I am truly in your debt and I look forward to many years of grateful repayment. And finally, to my husband, Tod, thank you for your love, support and understanding and being so proud of me and my accomplishment. Those long nights at the computer into the wee hours were worth it. Thanks for keeping the bed warm for me!

This book is dedicated to the medical staff, volunteers, patients and families at the University of Pittsburgh Medical Center/Passavant Hospital, Pittsburgh, PA. I am honored and privileged to be a part of their great work.